Pebble® Plus

How to Make Bubbles

Hands-On SCIENCE FUN

by Erika L. Shores

Consulting Editor: Gail Saunders-Smith, PhD

Consultant: Ronald Browne, PhD
Department of Elementary & Early Childhood Education
Minnesota State University, Mankato

CAPSTONE PRESS
a capstone imprint

Pebble Plus is published by Capstone Press,
151 Good Counsel Drive, P.O. Box 669, Mankato, Minnesota 56002.
www.capstonepub.com

Books published by Capstone Press are manufactured with paper
containing at least 10 percent post-consumer waste.

Library of Congress Cataloging-in-Publication Data
Shores, Erika L., 1976–
 How to make bubbles / by Erika L. Shores.
     p. cm.—(Pebble plus. Hands-on science fun)
 Summary: "Simple text and full-color photos instruct readers how to make bubbles and explain the science behind the
activity"—Provided by publisher.
 Includes bibliographical references and index.
 ISBN 978-1-4296-5293-3 (library binding)
 ISBN 978-1-4296-6215-4 (paperback)
 1. Soap bubbles—Experiments—Juvenile literature. 2. Science—Study and teaching (Preschool)—Activity
programs—Juvenile literature. 3. Surface tension—Experiments—Juvenile literature. I. Title. II. Series.
 QC183.S46 2011
 530.078—dc22   2010024910

Credits
Gene Bentdahl, designer; Sarah Schuette, photo shoot direction; Marcy Morin, scheduler;
    Laura Manthe, production specialist

Photo Credits
Capstone Studio/Karon Dubke, all

**The author dedicates this book to her mom, Betty Mikkelson, who has taught first graders
    at Lincoln Elementary School in Faribault, Minnesota, for 24 years.**

Note to Parents and Teachers

The Hands-On Science Fun series supports national science standards related to physical
science. This book describes and illustrates how to make soap bubbles. The images support
early readers in understanding the text. The repetition of words and phrases helps early readers
learn new words. This book also introduces early readers to subject-specific vocabulary words,
which are defined in the Glossary section. Early readers may need assistance to read some
words and to use the Table of Contents, Glossary, Read More, Internet Sites, and Index sections
of the book.

Printed in the United States of America in North Mankato, Minnesota.
092010
005933CGS11

Table of Contents

Safety Note:
Please ask an adult for help
when making bubbles.

Getting Started

Bubbles float in the sink.
Bubbles pop in a glass
of soda. Mix together simple
ingredients and make
your own super bubbles.

Here's what you need:

1 gallon (4 L)
warm water

1 cup (240 mL)
dish soap

1 tablespoon (15 mL)
glycerin (sold at drugstores)

large plastic tub

spoon

wire coat hanger

drinking straw, potato masher,
spatula, or other utensils
with holes

pipe cleaners

Making Bubbles

Pour 1 gallon of warm water into a large plastic tub.

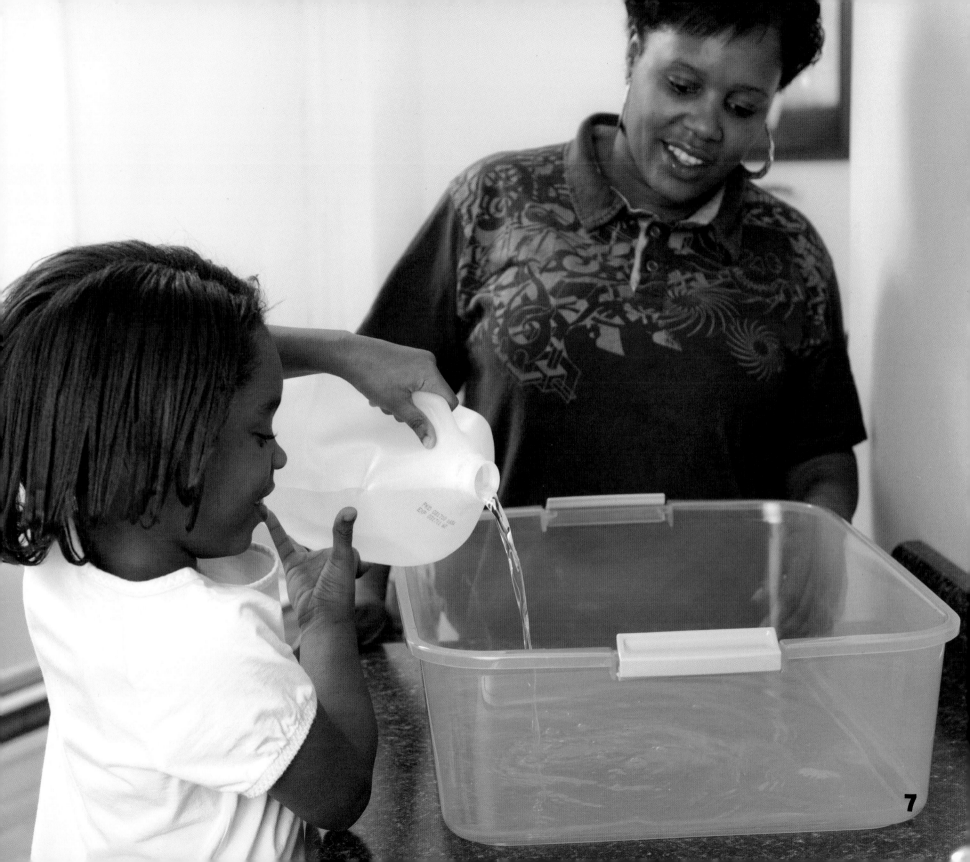

Add 1 cup of dish soap.

Next, add 1 tablespoon of glycerin.

Slowly stir the mixture.

Try not to make suds.

Let the bubble mixture
sit for two or three days.

Make your own bubble wand
by shaping a wire hanger
into a circle.

Wrap pipe cleaners
around the hanger.

Ask an adult to carry

the tub outside.

Blow lots of bubbles with a straw.

Dip a potato masher into the tub.

Blow through the holes.

Put the hanger into the mixture.

Pull it out slowly. Gently move it through the air.

You may have to try several times before you make a giant bubble.

How Does It Work?

Blowing air can make a thin film of soap stretch. When stretched too far, the film snaps closed. Air trapped inside makes a round bubble.

Bubbles burst when they dry out.
The soapy film gets too thin
and the air inside escapes.
A bubble also breaks when
it touches something dry.

Glossary

burst—to break apart suddenly

escape—to get away from

film—a very thin layer of something

glycerin—a syrupy liquid used in soaps, perfumes, and other products

ingredient—an item used to make something else

mixture—something made up of different things mixed together

Read More

Levine, Shar, and Leslie Johnstone. *The Ultimate Bubble Book: Soapy Science Fun.* New York: Sterling Pub. Co., 2003.

Tocci, Salvatore. *Experiments with Soap.* A True Book. New York: Children's Press, 2003.

Internet Sites

FactHound offers a safe, fun way to find Internet sites related to this book. All of the sites on FactHound have been researched by our staff.

Here's all you do:

Visit *www.facthound.com*

Type in this code: 9781429652933

Check out projects, games and lots more at
www.capstonekids.com

Index

Word Count: 189

Grade: 1

Early-Intervention Level: 18